WINDOWS OF COMFORT

(Two Organbooks)

Organbook I

by

Dan Locklair

978-0-7935-8182-5

e. c. kerby ltd.

DISTRIBUTED BY

HAL•LEONARD®
CORPORATION

7777 W. BLUEMOUND RD. P.O. BOX 13819 MILWAUKEE, WI 53213

WINDOWS OF COMFORT
Two Organbooks
by
Dan Locklair (b.1949)

Louis Comfort Tiffany (1848-1933), the American painter, stained-glass artist and glass manufacturer, created ten windows for the First Presbyterian Church of Topeka, Kansas, and they were installed in 1911. The windows are made of Favrile glass, a unique type of glass developed by Tiffany at his Tiffany Studios and Furnaces in New York. Not relying on paint for colour, Favrile glass instills its vibrant and jewelled colour palette directly into the glass itself. Viewed up close, the windows appear to be a kaleidoscopic array of colourful, precious stones. The secret to Tiffany's highly guarded, secret process for creating Favrile glass has never been divulged.

In the teaching spirit of the earliest Christian cathedral and church windows, the Tiffany windows of First Presbyterian Church use Biblical stories as their subjects. Except for the two Medallion Windows (where Trinitarian words and symbols are present), related scripture appears on each window.

In the pieces that make up the two organbooks of **WINDOWS OF COMFORT**, Mr. Tiffany's windows and their Bible texts have served as extra-musical stimuli. The stimuli for each piece came from a variety of dimensions, ranging from the impact of the smallest detail to the sheer drama of the complete window itself. Although each of the two organbooks is tightly knit within itself to allow each one to be played as a five-movement suite, it is also my intention that pieces from each organbook may be excerpted and grouped as the performer sees fit for recital or service of worship.

I wish to express my gratitude to all of the members of Topeka's First Presbyterian Church for their desire to celebrate, through this commission of music, their extraordinary Tiffany windows. Dr. Marie Rubis Bauer (First Presbyterian's organist) and Dr. Neil Weatherhogg (First Presbyterian's pastor) merit high and warm praise for their vision and resolve that has brought about the creation of **WINDOWS OF COMFORT**. Since I had the opportunity to view these windows prior to beginning work on this piece, I can attest to both their unique and stunning beauty as well as their Spiritual power.

SOLI DEO GLORIA!

To the performer:
Suggested registrations are given for a four-manual organ (the type found in Topeka's First Presbyterian Church). Manual indications are as follows: I = Choir; II = Great; III = Swell; IV = Solo (or Bombarde). The piece is conceived so that the performer may easily adapt **WINDOWS OF COMFORT** to either a two or three-manual instrument.

Organbook I

1. Trinity's Shield
Window: *The Shield of the Blessed Trinity* (one of two Medallion Windows)
The opening movement is based on only three pitches: E-flat, A-flat, B-flat. This exuberant piece not only numerically pays tribute to the Three-in-One, but, through crisp "rocks" of sound, acknowledges the "rocks" of jewelled glass that are at the heart of Tiffany's stunning creations.

2. "As the hart panteth..." [Passacaglia]
Window: *Psalm XLII* (*"As the hart panteth after the water brooks, so panteth my soul after Thee, O God."* Psalm 42:1)
The passacaglia melody (heard twelve times on the same 4' pedal stop), symbolizing "...so panteth my soul after Thee...", consists of ten different pitches in alternating duple (2) and triple (3) metre spanning five measures. The sustained left-hand part adds at each new variation one of the ten pitches on which the piece is based, symbolizing the ever-present sustaining power of God through the image of water. The right-hand's chromatic melody (always consisting of the ten pitches on which the piece is based), symbolizes the wandering of the hart as it searches for life-restoring waters.

3. "...the heavens were opened..." [Baptism Dance]
Window: *Baptism* (*"This is my beloved Son, in whom I am well pleased."* St. Matthew 3:17)
The radiant first part of this movement, featuring rhythmical dialogues between the pedal and manuals and between the manuals themselves, seeks to depict, through the spirit of energetic dance, the image of Christ going "...up straightway out of the water, and lo, the heavens were opened unto Him..." (St. Matthew 3:16). Culminating in a climax marked by a brilliant downward pedal solo, the vibrant first part of this piece melts into a still and serene second section symbolizing "the spirit of God descending like a dove, and lighting upon Him."

4. "...beside the still waters." [Chaconne]
Window: *Psalm XXIII* (*"The Lord is My Shepherd"*)
There are five statements of the twelve-measure chaconne, with the first four being rooted on the note "C" and the final one being centred on "D". A serene and lyrical movement, this piece is a reflection upon the peace of "...the still waters...".

5. Alpha and Omega
Window: *The North Medallion Window* (*"I am Alpha and Omega, the beginning and the end, the first and the last."* Revelation 22:13)
Like Movement 1 containing elements of The Trinity, this movement reflects back on both Movement 1 and Movement 3. Based on the same energetic three-note (E-flat, A-flat, B-flat) idea of number 1, this movement expands the pitch palette to include a half-step transposition of those pitches to E-natural, A-natural, B-natural. Similar to the two-part structure of Movement 3, the broad musical idea that symbolized the dove's descent in number 3 returns in the second part of Movement 5, only here it is presented with the strength of full organ. The fast tempo that opened it, returns to close the movement.

Organbook I timings: 1. ca. **2'**; 2. ca. **4'**; 3. ca. **3'30"**; 4. ca. **4'**; 5. ca. **3'30"**   Total duration: ca. 17 minutes

Dan Locklair,
Winston-Salem, NC
Autumn, 1996

To obtain full-colour slides of the ten Tiffany windows which inspired **WINDOWS OF COMFORT**, write to:
First Presbyterian Church, 817 SW Harrison St., Topeka, KS 66612 USA or call (913) 233-9601

*Commissioned by the First Presbyterian Church, Topeka, Kansas
in celebration of ten windows by Louis Comfort Tiffany in the
First Presbyterian Church sanctuary and dedicated to its pastor, Dr. Neil Weatherhogg, 1996*

Windows of Comfort
Organbook I

Dan Locklair

*Suggested registration:
I,II, III:
Founds., reeds 16', 8', 4' 2', mixs.
All manuals coupled.
Ped: Founds., reeds 16', 8', 4', mixs.,
I,II, III to ped.

1. Trinity's Shield

* N.B. All manual **I** indications may be
performed on an antiphonal division if
available and if acoustics allow it.

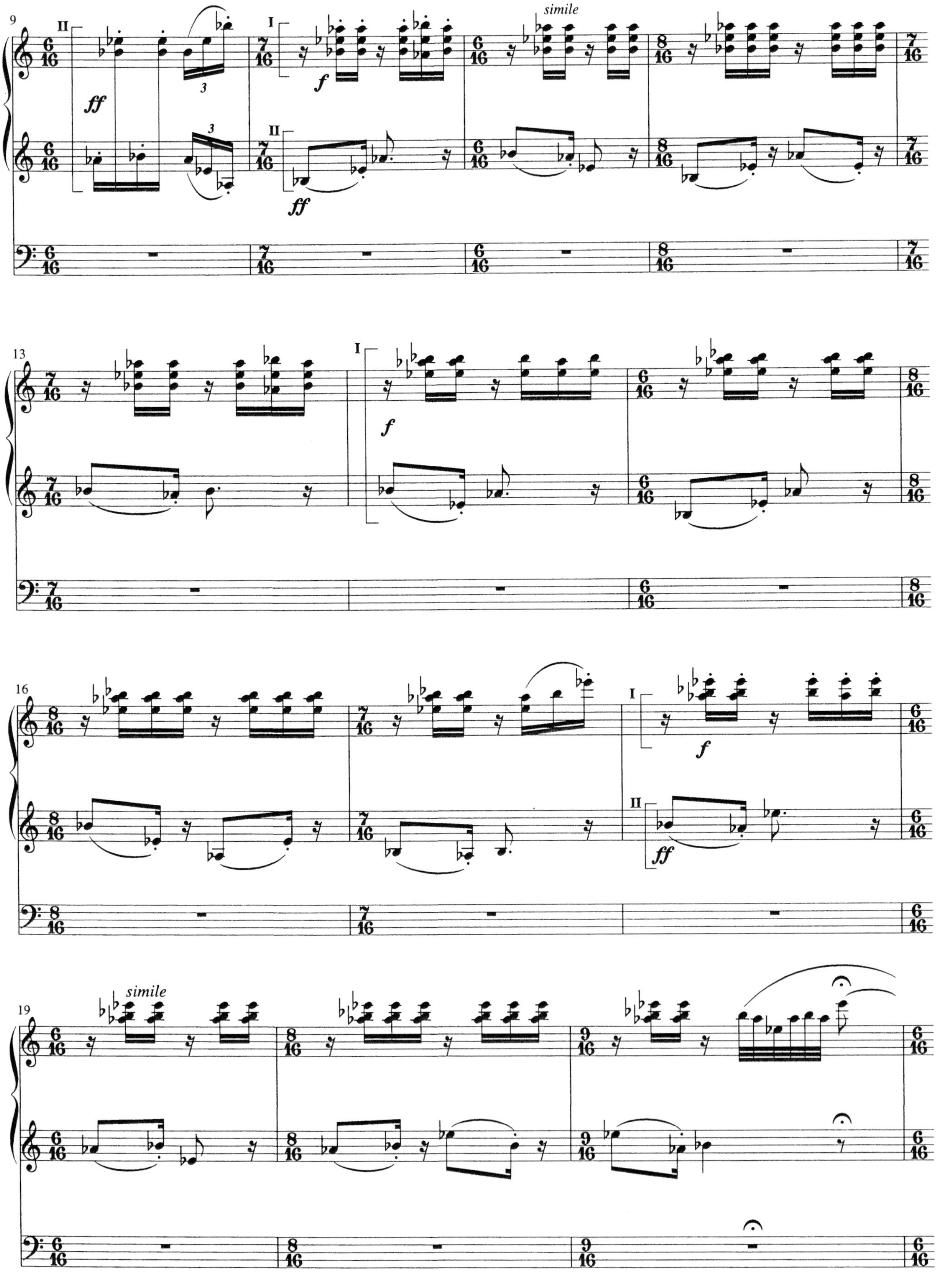
9
II
I
simile
ff
f
13
16
19
simile

6

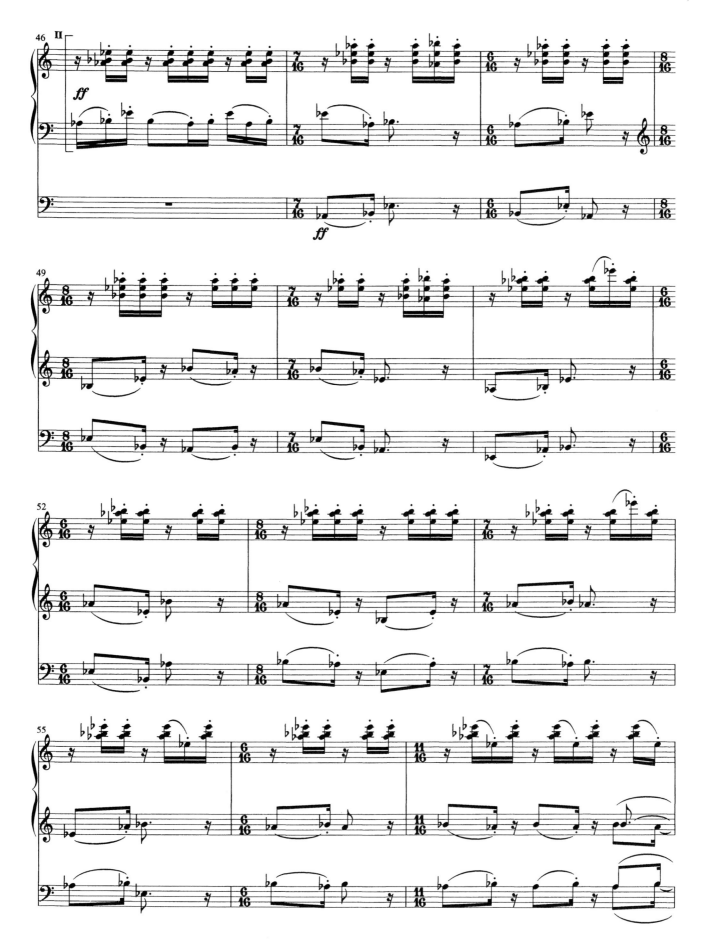

8

(may add)

*IV
(or II)

ff

* If an antiphonal division is available and used,
  it may be coupled here to the front division.

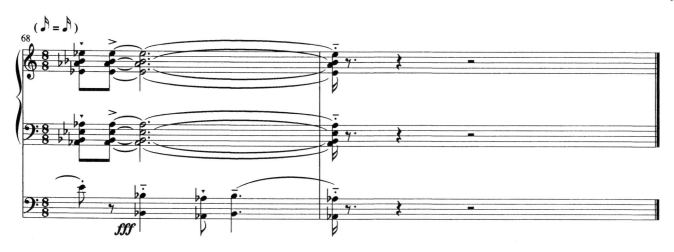

2. "As the hart panteth..." [Passacaglia]
(Psalm 42)

*Suggested registration:
I (or II): Solo 8' colour, opt. tremolo
III: Celeste strings
Ped: Flute (or diapason) 4'

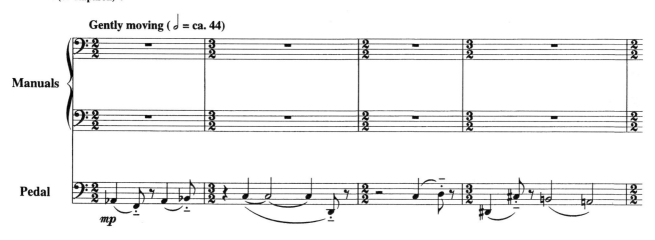

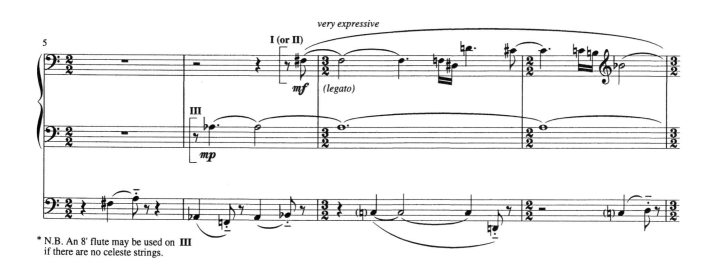

* N.B. An 8' flute may be used on **III**
if there are no celeste strings.

10

12

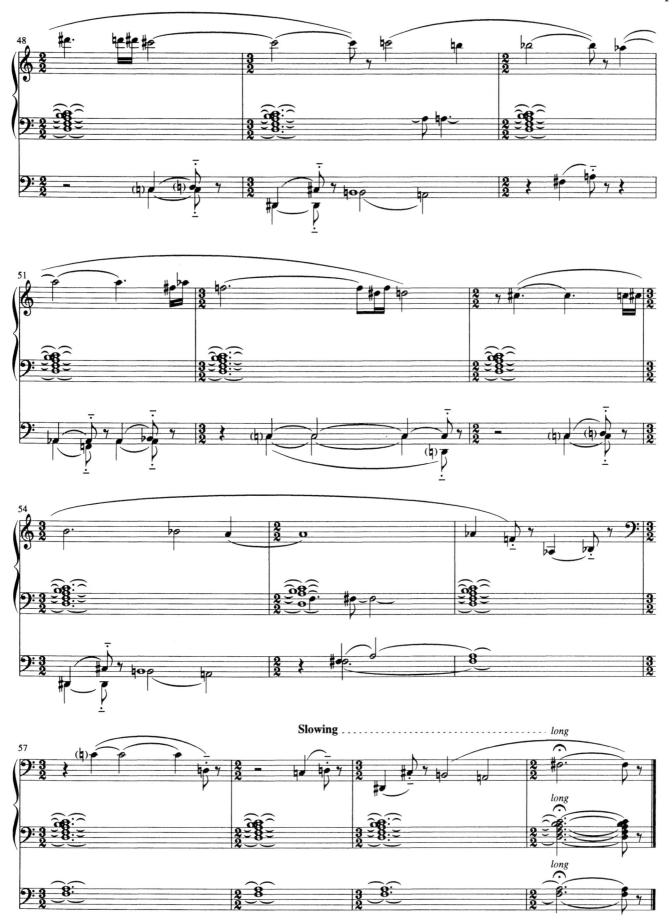

3. "...the heavens were opened..."
(Baptism Dance)

*Suggested registration:
I, II, III:
Founds., reeds 16', 8', 4', 2', mixs.
All manuals coupled.
IV: Large 8'reed
Ped: Founds., reeds 16', 8', 4', mixs.
Manuals coupled to ped.

*May also be played on an antiphonal division if available.

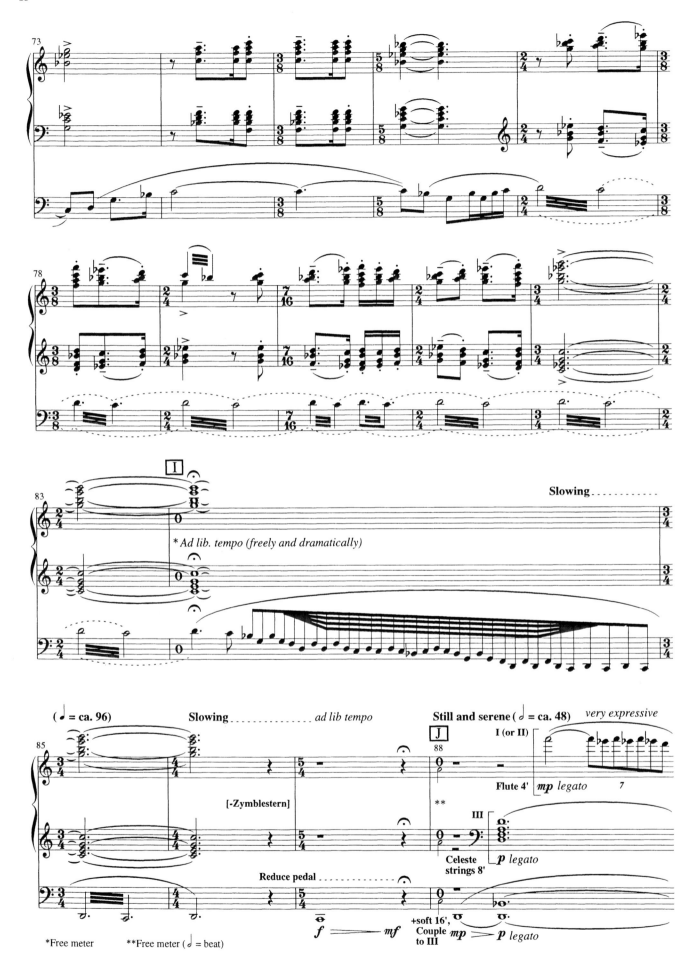

*Free meter **Free meter (𝅗𝅥 = beat)

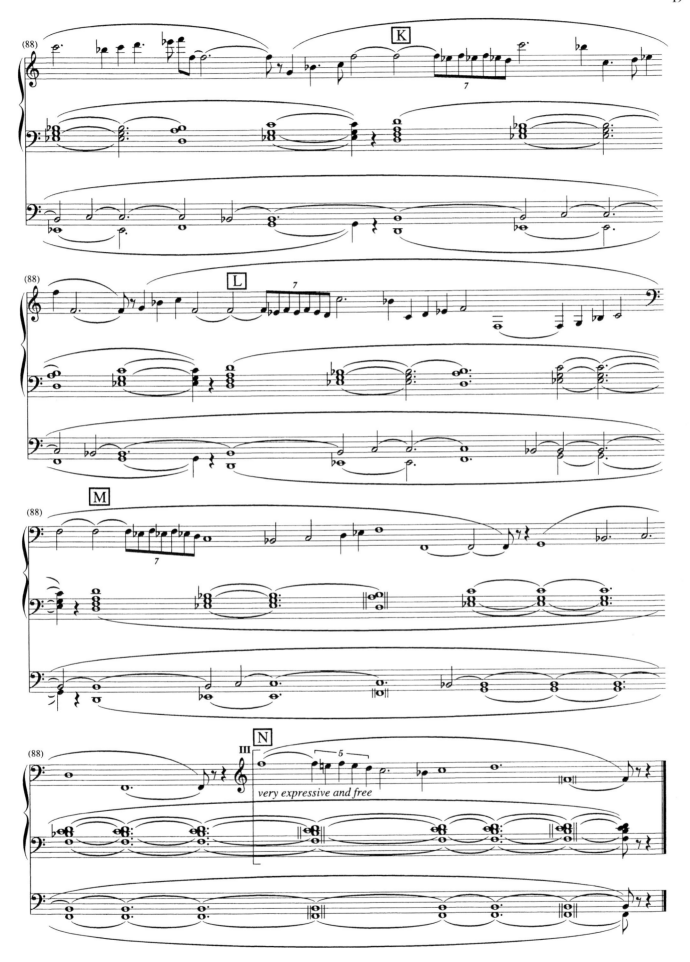

4. "...beside the still waters." [Chaconne]
(Psalm 23)

Suggested registration:
I: Flute 4' (Fl. 4' may, instead, be registered on II)
II: Diapason 8'
III: Flute (or string) celestes 8'
Ped: III to ped.

Broaden

In tempo

5. Alpha and Omega

*Suggested registration:
 I, II, III, IV:
 Founds., reeds 16', 8', 4', 2', mixs.
 All manuals coupled.
 Ped. Founds., reeds 16', 8', 4', I and III to Ped.

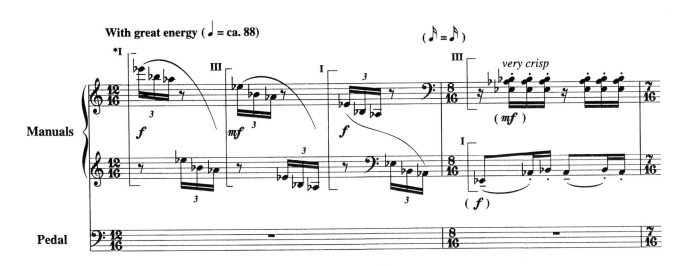

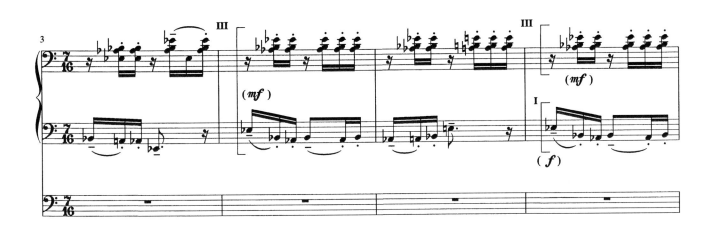

*On two-manual organs, dialoguing sections throughout
 may be alternated between **II** and **III** or (until m. 18) may just be played on **III**.

(add II to ped.) **ff**

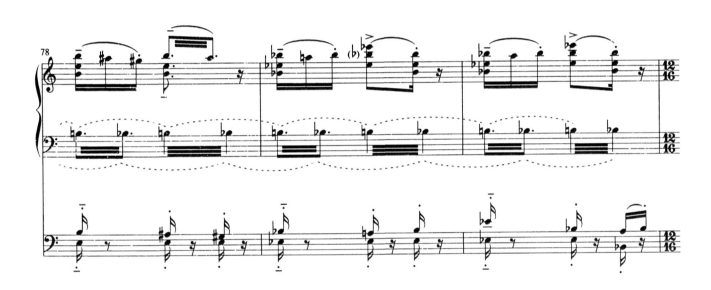

Broaden

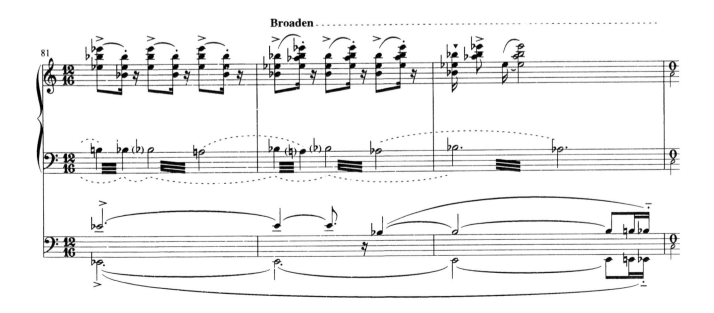

32

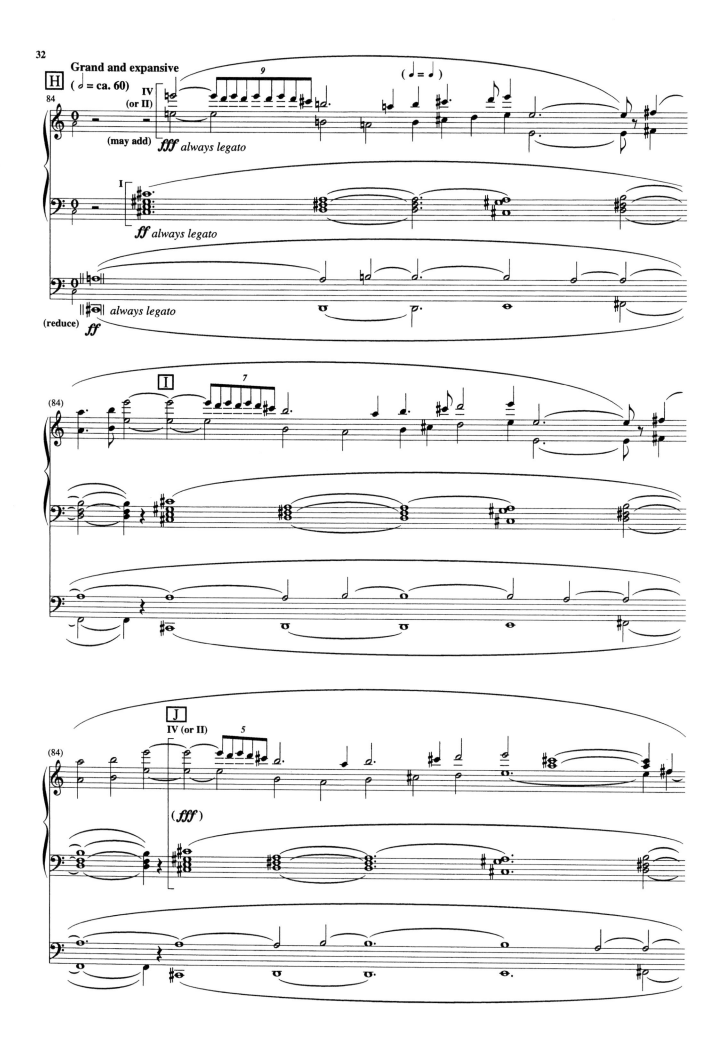

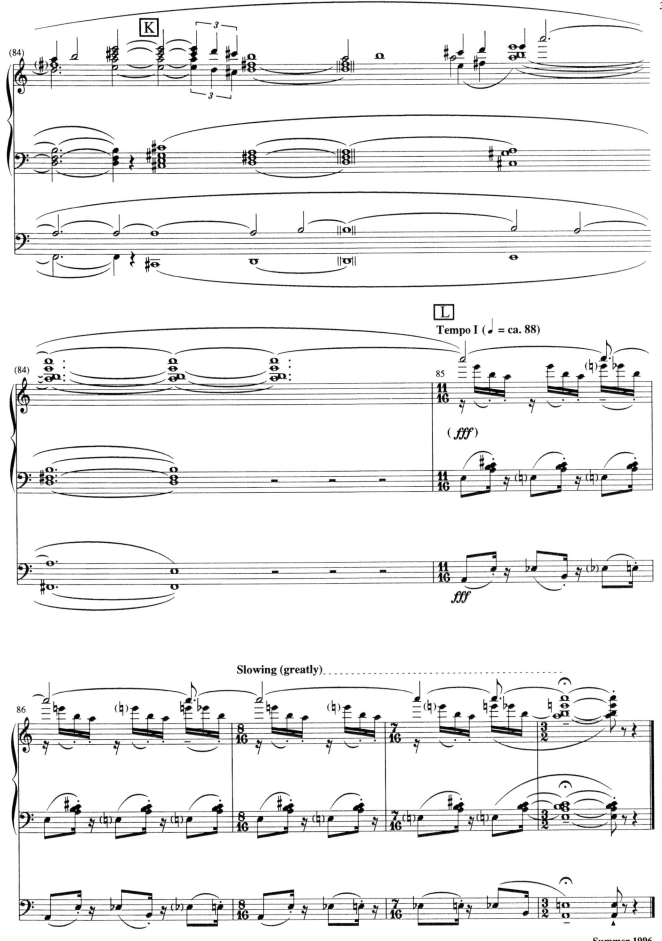

Summer 1996
Winston-Salem, NC